This book belongs to

Kurt R. Boyles

STORIES ABOUT JESUS

KENNETH N. TAYLOR

Illustrated by Nancy Munger

TYNDALE HOUSE PUBLISHERS, INC.   WHEATON, ILLINOIS

Library of Congress Cataloging-in-Publication Data

Taylor, Kenneth Nathaniel.
        Stories about Jesus / Kenneth N. Taylor ; illustrated by Nancy Munger.
            p.   cm.
        Text and illustrations adapted from author's Good news for little people. Scripture verses from
    The Bible for children (The Simplified Living Bible).
        ISBN 0-8423-6093-X
        1. Jesus Christ—Biography—Juvenile literature.   2. Bible stories, English—N.T. Gospels.
    3. Children—Prayer-books and devotions—English.   [1. Jesus Christ—Biography.   2. Bible
    stories—N.T.   3. Prayer books and devotions.]   I. Munger, Nancy, ill.   II. Taylor, Kenneth
    Nathaniel. Good news for little people.   III. Bible. English. Simplified Living Bible. 1994. IV. Title.
    BT302.T263   1994
    232.9'01—dc20   94-4083
    [B]

Printed in Singapore

99   98   97   96   95   94
10   9   8   7   6   5   4   3   2   1

PREFACE
(To be read by parents and grandparents)

Jesus loves me
This I know
For the Bible
Tells me so

This little song is filled with great truths. How important it is for even the smallest child to know that he or she is loved. And how wonderful to grow up knowing the love of Jesus.

How will the child learn about this beautiful fact? "The Bible tells me so." Yes, God has told us in the Bible about Jesus' love for little people—as well as for their parents and grandparents.

This book tells in simple language the stories about Jesus—how He walked on the water to rescue His friends, how He brought a twelve-year-old girl back to life, and how He healed many people who were very sick. These are true stories every child needs to know. For at a very young age a child can learn not only that Jesus loves us but also to love Him in return.

That is the purpose of this book.

KENNETH N. TAYLOR

P.S. Don't forget to look for the ladybugs on many of the pages!

An Angel Brings Good News to Mary

The angel came to Mary
With news of wondrous joy:
She was going to have a baby,
And He would be God's boy!

Here is a picture of an angel telling Mary some exciting news. God sent the angel to tell her that she would have a baby. Her baby would look like any other baby, but He would be God's Son. The angel told Mary to name her baby Jesus. He would be our Savior.

Some Questions to Answer
1. What would be the baby's name?
2. Who is Jesus' father?

A Little Prayer

Dear Father in heaven, thank You for sending Jesus to save us.

A Bible Verse for You to Say

His Kingdom shall never end! LUKE 1:33

The Angels
Tell the Good News
to the Shepherds

The sheep and little lambs look up.
The sky is filled with light.
The angels sing to shepherds
Of Jesus' birth that night.

Look at all the angels in the sky. They have come to tell good news to the men taking care of the sheep. God sent the angels to tell the men that His Son, Jesus, was born that night in the town of Bethlehem.

Some Questions to Answer
1. What did the angels tell the men?
2. What is the name of the town where Jesus was born?

A Little Prayer

Thank You, God, for Your Son, Jesus. Thank You that He is our Savior.

A Bible Verse for You to Say

I bring you the most joyful news ever told! The Savior has been born tonight in Bethlehem!

LUKE 2:10-11

The Shepherds Worship Jesus

Away in a manger,
No crib for a bed,
The little Lord Jesus
Laid down His sweet head.

The shepherds hurried to the nearby town of Bethlehem. They found the baby Jesus with Mary, His mother. Was He born in a hospital? No, it was in a place where cows and donkeys stayed. He was warmly wrapped in strips of cloth and was lying in a box filled with dry grass. What a strange place for the Son of God to be born! The shepherds thanked God for sending His Son to be our Savior.

Some Questions to Answer

1. What kind of place was Jesus born in?
2. Where was baby Jesus lying when the shepherds came?

A Little Prayer

Dear Jesus, thank You for becoming a baby. Thank You for coming to save me.

A Bible Verse for You to Say

God loved the world so much that he gave his only Son. JOHN 3:16

The Wise Men Follow the Star to Jesus

The wise men came from far away
To greet the newborn King.
They knelt before Him and they said,
"Our gifts to You we bring."

Can you see Jesus with Joseph and Mary? How many wise men do you see? Can you see their camels? The wise men are bringing presents to Jesus. Why did they bring Him gifts? It is because Jesus is God's Son from heaven, and the wise men have come to kneel down and worship Him.

Some Questions to Answer

1. Whose son is Jesus?
2. Why did the wise men bring gifts to Jesus?
   Because Jesus is God's Son.

A Little Prayer

Dear God, help me to know how great and good You are. Help me always to want to give You some of my good things.

A Bible Verse for You to Say

The wise men threw themselves down before him, worshiping. MATTHEW 2:11

Jesus Grows Up

The grown-ups stood and listened
To the questions Jesus raised.
This boy had so much wisdom
That they were all amazed.

In this picture Jesus is twelve years old. Can you see Him talking to the old men? He is telling them about God and answering their questions. They are surprised because He knows so much about heaven. He knew all about it because He had always been there with God His Father before He was born.

Some Questions to Answer

1. Who is Jesus talking to the men about?
2. Where was Jesus before He was born? *In heaven with God, His Father.*

A Little Prayer

Dear Father in heaven, thank You for Your Son, Jesus. Thank You that He is my friend.

A Bible Verse for You to Say

So Jesus grew both tall and wise. And he was loved by both God and man. LUKE 2:52

Jesus Calls His Disciples

Jesus calls His disciples—

At first a pair of brothers,

Then ten more men, and you,
    and me,

And many, many others.

Jesus has grown up and become a man. He is telling these two men to come with Him and be His helpers. They said yes and got out of the water and went with Him. Jesus wants you to be His helper too. How wonderful that is. Do you want to be His helper? You can pray and tell Him so.

Some Questions to Answer
1. Do you want to be Jesus' helper?
2. How can you tell Him so? *By talking to Him in prayer.*

A Little Prayer

Dear Jesus, thank You for asking me to be Your special friend.

A Bible Verse for You to Say

Jesus called out, "Come along with me! . . ." They left their nets at once and went with him.

MATTHEW 4:19-20

Jesus Makes a Dead Girl Well

This little girl got sick and died,

But Jesus came and said,

"Get up, dear child, and run
and play."

Then she jumped out of bed!

See how happy the kitties are! The girl's mother and father and brother and sisters are happy too! Do you know why everyone is so happy? It is because Jesus told the girl to come back to life, and she did. Just before Jesus came to her house, she was dead. Now you can see she is all well again.

Some Questions to Answer
1. Was the little girl dead?
2. Who brought her back to life again?

A Little Prayer

Dear Jesus, thank You for making the girl alive after she was dead. Thank You for making her family happy again.

A Bible Verse for You to Say

Taking her by the hand he said to her, "Get up, little girl!" . . . And she jumped up and walked around! MARK 5:41-42

Through the Roof

He couldn't move his hands
    or feet,

He couldn't move at all.

Then Jesus said, "Get up and walk!"

He did, and didn't fall.

Why is this man so happy?
Why is he dancing around?
A few minutes ago he couldn't
walk at all. His friends carried
him on that hammock. They
cut a hole in the flat roof
and lowered him down to
Jesus. You can see his friends
looking through the roof.
Then Jesus told the man to be
all right again, and suddenly
he was healed. That is why
he is so happy.

Some Questions to Answer

1. Why is the man so happy?
2. How did his friends get him down in front
   of Jesus?

A Little Prayer

Dear Jesus, thank You for making the man walk. Thank You for all the wonderful things You do.

A Bible Verse for You to Say

He said to the man, "My friend, your sins are forgiven!" LUKE 5:20

Jesus and Little Children

Jesus loves the little children,

All the children of the
world.

Red and yellow,
black and white,

They are precious
in His sight.

Jesus loves the
little children
of the world.

The man wearing a green hat and striped shirt is telling some fathers and mothers to take their children away. He said Jesus was too busy to talk to children. But Jesus told the man not to send the children away, because He loves children! The children came to Jesus, and He blessed each one.

Some Questions to Answer
1. Is Jesus too busy to talk to children?
2. How can you talk to Him?

A Little Prayer

Thank You, God, for loving me. Thank You that Jesus doesn't say, "Go away." Thank You that I can come to Jesus so He can bless me.

A Bible Verse for You to Say

Jesus said, "Let the little children come to me. Don't stop them." MATTHEW 19:14

Jesus Heals a Blind Man

The man is blind,
  he cannot see.

He cannot use his eyes.

But Jesus came and made
  him well.

What a wonderful surprise!

Shut your eyes and walk across the room. What would it be like if you couldn't see? This man couldn't ever see at all. He was blind. Then Jesus came. "Do you believe I can make you see?" Jesus asked him. The man said yes. Then Jesus touched the man's eyes, and look! He can see! He believed in Jesus, and Jesus made him well.

Some Questions to Answer

1. Did the blind man think Jesus could make him see?
2. What did Jesus do?

A Little Prayer

Jesus, thank You because I can see the beautiful things You made. Thank You, thank You, thank You.

A Bible Verse for You to Say

Jesus said, "All right, begin seeing! Your faith has healed you." LUKE 18:42

The Good Samaritan

A man lay bleeding by the road.

Some people passed him by.

But one man stopped and
    helped him,

And didn't let him die.

This man was badly hurt by some robbers. They took all of his money and ran away. Some men came along and saw him lying there, but they didn't help him. You can see them walking away. But now someone who doesn't like him is helping him. If you saw someone get hurt, I hope you would stop and help. That is what Jesus wants you to do.

Some Questions to Answer
1. What happened to the man lying there?
2. Who is helping him? *A man who doesn't like him.*

A Little Prayer

Dear Father in heaven, thank You that the Good Samaritan helped the man who was hurt. Help me to be a helper too.

A Bible Verse for You to Say

When he saw the man, he felt deep pity.

LUKE 10:33

Jesus Feeds Five Thousand People

A little boy had brought his lunch—
Two fish, five loaves of bread.
In Jesus' hands it grew until
The hungry crowd
    was fed.

These people were hungry! They had come to hear Jesus. Now it was late, and they didn't have enough food. One boy had five pieces of bread and two small fish. He offered them to Jesus, and Jesus did a miracle! He made the boy's lunch become enough food for everyone! And there were several basketfuls left over!

Some Questions to Answer

1. What did the boy have in his lunch?
2. Who did he give them to? Then what happened?

A Little Prayer

Thank You, God, for giving Jesus the power to make the bread and fish become enough for everyone.

A Bible Verse for You to Say

He gives food to the hungry. PSALM 146:7

Jesus Makes a Dead Man Live Again

Jesus' friend named Lazarus

Got very sick and died.

But Jesus came and called
to him—

And then he came to life.

The man wrapped in strips of cloth is named Lazarus. He died and was buried by being put in the stone tomb you can see behind him. He was a friend of Jesus, and Jesus came and called out to him, "Lazarus, come out!" Right away Lazarus stopped being dead and walked out of the tomb, all well again! Jesus can do wonderful things!

Some Questions to Answer
1. What did Jesus say to Lazarus?
2. Then what did Lazarus do?

A Little Prayer

Thank You, God, for making Lazarus alive and well again. Thank You for Your great power.

A Bible Verse for You to Say

He shouted, "Lazarus, come out!" And Lazarus came out! JOHN 11:43-44

Jesus Walks on Water

Who can walk on water?
It just cannot be done!
But Jesus did it easily—
He is the only One.

Jesus' friends were in a boat when a big storm came along. Jesus wasn't with them. He walked out from the beach to help them. Look! He is walking on top of the water! His friends in the boat were frightened. They thought Jesus was a ghost! But Jesus called out to them, "It's Me! Don't be afraid!" Then they were excited and happy.

Some Questions to Answer

1. Can you walk on top of water?
2. Why could Jesus do this? *He was the Son of God.*

A Little Prayer

Thank You, God, for the wonderful things Jesus can do. Thank You that He will use His great power to help me.

A Bible Verse for You to Say

"It's all right," he said. "It is I! Don't be afraid."

MARK 6:50

Jesus Makes All the People Well

The people came from all around—

All weak and sick and sad.

But Jesus' touch has made
them well.

They're thankful now,
and glad!

These people were all sick or blind or couldn't walk or had other things wrong with them. But Jesus is healing them. You can see how happy they are. Some of them are still waiting for Jesus to touch them and make them well. Jesus will heal them all.

Some Questions to Answer
1. Why are the sick people coming to Jesus?
2. What happened to the sick people?

A Little Prayer

Thank You, Jesus, for making all those people well. Thank You for caring about how we feel.

A Bible Verse for You to Say

When he spoke a single word, all the demons left. And all the sick were healed. MATTHEW 8:16

Jesus Prays

Jesus talks to His Father.

His Father is God above.

You, too, can talk to His
    Father—

He listens to you with love.

Jesus is praying. He is talking to God, who made all the birds and animals. God is His Father. God the Father loves to have His Son, Jesus, talk to Him. You can't see God in the picture, but He is listening. You and I can talk to God too. He likes us to do this and listens to us because He loves us.

Some Questions to Answer
1. What is Jesus doing?
2. Can children talk to God?

A Little Prayer

Dear God, thank You that I can talk to You. Thank You for listening to me. Help me to listen to what You tell me.

A Bible Verse for You to Say

Pray for each other. JAMES 5:16

Jesus Stops the Storm

The storm was wild, the waves
were high,

Disciples feared that
they would die.

But Jesus spoke,
the wind
stopped blowing,

The boat arrived
where it
was going.

Jesus was in the boat with His friends when a bad storm came along. He was asleep in the back of the boat, but His friends woke Him up. "Lord, save us!" they screamed. "We're sinking." But Jesus stood up and said to the wind, "Quiet down," and He told the waves to go away. Then everything was all right again. Now at last His friends knew He was God's Son.

Some Questions to Answer
1. Why were the men so frightened?
2. What did Jesus do?

A Little Prayer

How wonderful, Lord Jesus, that You can make the storms go away.

A Bible Verse for You to Say

Why were you so afraid? Don't you have confidence in me yet? MARK 4:40

Jesus Makes Ten Men Well

Jesus made the sick men well—
Count them, one to ten.
How many men said
 thank you?
Just one came back again.

Can you count these ten happy men? They all had the same bad sickness, and Jesus healed them all. You can see how happy they are because they are well again. But do you know what they forgot? They forgot to say, "Thank You, Jesus, for making me well." Only one of them remembered to say thank you. Can you point to him?

Some Questions to Answer

1. When someone is kind to you, do you say thank you?
2. Name some ways Jesus has been kind to you. *Giving you a home, parents, food, having Jesus as your friend. . . .* What else?

A Little Prayer

Thank You, Jesus, for healing the ten men who were sick. Thank You for all the kind things You do for me.

A Bible Verse for You to Say

One of them came back to Jesus. . . . He thanked Jesus for what he had done. LUKE 17:15-16

The People Welcome Jesus

"Glory to God!"
    the people shout.

"Glory!" the children sing.

They wave the palms and
    spread their coats

To show He is their king!

All the people are happy because they want Jesus to be their king. They are putting their clothes and blankets on the ground like a carpet in front of His donkey. And they are waving palm branches. This is the way the people showed how much they liked Jesus.

Some Questions to Answer

1. Why are the children waving palm branches? *To show Jesus that they want Him to be their king.*
2. What can we do to show Jesus that we love Him? *We can thank Him in our prayers.*

A Little Prayer

Dear Jesus, thank You for being my great and good King. I want You to be in charge of my life.

A Bible Verse for You to Say

God has given us a King! . . . Glory to God in the highest Heavens! LUKE 19:38

Jesus Is Arrested

Judas was Jesus' disciple,
But Judas was sneaky and sly.
He acted as if he loved Jesus,
But really he hoped He
     would die.

Oh, no! What is happening here? Some soldiers have come to arrest Jesus. Did He do something wrong? No, He always did what was right and good. But some men didn't like Him, so they sent the soldiers to take Jesus away and kill Him.

Some Questions to Answer
1. What are the soldiers doing?
2. Did Jesus do something wrong?

A Little Prayer

Jesus, I am sorry Your friend turned against You. Help me never to turn against You.

A Bible Verse for You to Say

He prayed, "My Father! . . . I want what you want. I will do your will, not mine." MATTHEW 26:39

Jesus Forgives Peter

How could you do it, Peter?
How could you hurt your friend?
Yet Jesus said, "I forgive you."
Even this sin He could mend.

Peter is running away. He is one of Jesus' best friends, but he is afraid the soldiers will hurt him if they find out. So he told everyone that he didn't even know Jesus! Jesus looked at Peter, and Peter began to cry. He loved Jesus, but he told a lie to keep from getting hurt.

Some Questions to Answer
1. Was Peter one of Jesus' friends?
2. Why did Peter say he didn't know Jesus?

A Little Prayer

Dear God, please help me never, ever to turn against my friend Jesus like Peter did.

A Bible Verse for You to Say

Satan has asked to have you. . . . But I have begged in prayer for you. LUKE 22:31-32

Jesus Dies on the Cross

Up there on the hill I see
Jesus' cross, at Calvary.
Jesus died for you and me.
Jesus died to set us free.

They are killing Jesus by nailing Him to a cross. This is called the crucifixion of Jesus. You and I have done wrong things, so we deserve to be punished by God. But in this picture we can see God punishing Jesus for our sins. Now God doesn't need to punish us. How kind of Jesus to be willing to be punished in our place.

Some Questions to Answer

1. What did Jesus do to save you from God's punishment? *He died in your place so God can forgive you.*
2. Have you thanked Jesus for dying for you? Let's do it now.

A Little Prayer

Dear Jesus, thank You for dying for my sins. Help me to learn more and more about all You have done for me.

A Bible Verse for You to Say

Truly, this was the Son of God! MARK 15:39

Jesus Is Raised from the Dead

The night is past—
Look at the light!
Jesus is risen,
The world is bright!

Jesus died on the cross, but three days later God brought Him back to life again! Here He is talking to one of His friends. How surprised she is, and how happy. Jesus is alive! He died for our sins, but God didn't let Him stay dead. If we love Jesus, God will make us live again in heaven after we are dead!

Some Questions to Answer
1. Is Jesus dead or alive? *He is alive.*
2. Who made Him alive again? *God did.*

A Little Prayer

Thank You, Jesus, for dying for me. Thank You, God, for bringing Jesus back to life again. Thank You! Thank You! Thank You!

A Bible Verse for You to Say

He has come back to life again. MATTHEW 28:6

Jesus Helps His Friends Catch Fish

They fished all night
Without a bite,
Till Jesus came
And made things right.

One morning after God raised Jesus from the dead, His friends had gone fishing. They fished all night but couldn't catch anything. Jesus told them to put their fishing net on the other side of the boat. They did, and then they caught more than a hundred big fish!

Some Questions to Answer
1. What did Jesus tell His friends to do?
2. Then what happened?

A Little Prayer

Dear Jesus, help me to be like Your disciples and do whatever You tell me to.

A Bible Verse for You to Say

You are my friends if you obey me. JOHN 15:14

Jesus Goes to His Father

Jesus said, "For now, good-bye—
I'm going home, but please don't cry.
My Father's there, and angels too,
And someday I'll come back for you."

Look where Jesus is! He is going up into the clouds. He is going up to heaven where He came from. He is going back to God, His Father. Before He left His friends, He told them, "I will come back again." While Jesus is away, He thinks about us every day. He thinks about how much He loves us. He wants us to be with Him.

Some Questions to Answer
1. What is happening in this picture? *Jesus is rising into the sky.*
2. Where is He going? *To His Father, in heaven.*

A Little Prayer

Dear Jesus, please come soon.

A Bible Verse for You to Say

"Yes, I am coming soon!" Amen! Come, Lord Jesus! REVELATION 22:20

Jesus Will Come Back Again

Jesus went away to heaven,
And someday He'll return.
Oh, the joys that we will have,
The happy things we'll learn!

Here is a picture of Jesus coming back again! He will come to take us with Him to heaven. Then we will be with Him and all the other people who love Jesus. He will talk to us and take care of us. No one will ever be sick or get hurt in heaven. We will always be happy. Jesus wants us to tell everyone the good news that He died for them and is coming again to take us to be with Him forever.

Some Questions to Answer

1. What is happening in this picture? *Jesus is coming back to take us to heaven.*
2. If we love Jesus, will we go to be with Him in heaven?

A Little Prayer

Dear Jesus, we want to see You. We want to live with You. Thank You for loving us. Please come soon.

A Bible Verse for You to Say

Jesus has gone to Heaven. And someday he will come back again, just as he went! ACTS 1:11

ABOUT THE AUTHOR

Kenneth N. Taylor is best known as the translator of *The Living Bible,* but his first renown was as a writer of children's books. Ken and his wife, Margaret, have ten children, and his early books were written for use in the family's daily devotions. The manuscripts were ready for publication only when they passed the scrutiny of those ten young critics! Those books, which have now been read to two generations of children around the world, include *The Bible in Pictures for Little Eyes* (Moody Press), *Stories for the Children's Hour* (Moody Press), and *The Living Bible Story Book* (Tyndale House). Now the Taylor children are all grown, so *Stories about Jesus, Big Thoughts for Little People, Giant Steps for Little People,* and *Wise Words for Little People* are written with his twenty-eight grandchildren in mind.

Ken Taylor is a graduate of Wheaton College and Northern Baptist Seminary. He is the founder and chairman of Tyndale House Publishers. He and Margaret live in Wheaton, Illinois.

ABOUT THE ILLUSTRATOR

Nancy Munger, a free-lance illustrator, has prepared illustrations for many different media, including textbooks, book jackets, album covers, magazine articles, and advertisements. Books she has illustrated include *The NIV Children's Bible* and *The Adventure Bible* as well as several other children's books. She also enjoys using her talents in her church. A board member of the church's childcare program, she helps to raise money for it by selling Christian children's prints.

Nancy is a graduate of Ferris State University and the Art Center College of Design. She and her husband, Doug Anderson, live with their two children, Jessie and Joshua, on a farm near Delton, Michigan, where they enjoy their many ponies, horses, sheep, goats, chickens, and ducks. About this book Nancy says, "I treasure the time spent on this book because of the closeness I have felt to the Lord while working on it."